UFOs AND ALIENS

BY ARNOLD RINGSTAD

Published by The Child's World®
1980 Lookout Drive • Mankato, MN 56003-1705
800-599-READ • www.childsworld.com

Photographs ©: Shutterstock Images, cover, 1,
3, 10, 11; Cheri Alguire/Shutterstock Images, 2,
6, 7 (bottom); HQuality/Shutterstock Images,
4; Cracker Clips Stock Media/Shutterstock
Images, 7; Cloud One Photo/Shutterstock
Images, 8; Denis Moskvinov/Shutterstock
Images, 12; JPL-Caltech/Ames/NASA, 14–15;
MSFC/NASA, 16; JPL-Caltech/NASA, 18; ARC/
NASA, 19, 19 (inset); Red Line Editorial, 21;
Michael Vi/Shutterstock Images, 22 (top); Paulo
Afonso/Shutterstock Images, 22 (bottom)

ISBN 9781503844742 (Reinforced Library Binding)
ISBN 9781503846203 (Portable Document Format)
ISBN 9781503847392 (Online Multi-user eBook)
LCCN 2019957732

Printed in the United States of America

About the Author
Arnold Ringstad loves reading
about space science and
exploration. He lives in Minnesota
with his wife and their cat.

CONTENTS

CHAPTER ONE
LIFE IN SPACE? . . . 5

CHAPTER TWO
WHAT IS A UFO? . . . 9

CHAPTER THREE
SEARCHING FOR LIFE . . . 13

CHAPTER FOUR
TALKING TO ALIENS . . . 17

OUT OF THIS WORLD! . . . 22

GLOSSARY . . . 23

TO LEARN MORE . . . 24

INDEX . . . 24

LIFE IN SPACE?

Are we alone? People on Earth have been asking this question for hundreds of years. Scientists study space for signs of life. Writers create stories about aliens. Some fictional aliens are peaceful. Others try to take over Earth.

The way many people think about aliens changed in 1947. Two events happened that summer. First, an American pilot named Kenneth Arnold saw something strange in the sky. He was flying in Washington state. He said he saw nine glowing objects flying above a mountain. He said they moved like "a saucer if you skip it across water." Some people mistakenly thought he meant he saw saucer-shaped objects.

◄ Many works of science fiction imagine life with aliens. Some imagine humans and aliens living and working together peacefully.

Some people believe an alien ship ▶
crashed in Roswell, New Mexico.
The small town is now
associated with aliens.

Soon, other people around the country were reporting that they also saw strange things in the sky. Similar reports have continued ever since.

Later that summer, a newspaper in Roswell, New Mexico, published an unusual story. It said that the army had found a crashed flying saucer near Roswell. The army said it was actually a crashed weather balloon.

Few people paid attention to the story at first. But in the 1970s, some people began saying an alien ship had crashed near Roswell. There was no evidence for this. Still, flying saucers and aliens became linked with that city.

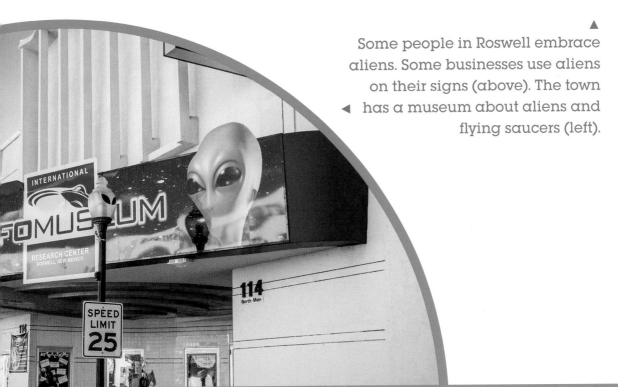

Some people in Roswell embrace aliens. Some businesses use aliens on their signs (above). The town has a museum about aliens and flying saucers (left).

CHAPTER TWO

WHAT IS A UFO?

People continued to report strange objects in the sky. These became known as unidentified flying objects (UFOs). The U.S. government studied UFO sightings in the 1950s and 1960s. Some people worried UFOs could be aircraft from enemy countries. But the government found that this was not the case. The government kept its reports about UFOs secret for many years. This made some people think the government was hiding discoveries about aliens.

◄ Many people think the U.S. government is hiding secrets about aliens in a place called Area 51. This top-secret air force base is located in Nevada.

▲
Because meteors move across the night sky,
people might think they're seeing a UFO.

Some people think UFOs are alien ships. But there are many explanations for strange things in the sky. They may be secret military rockets or planes. Governments would not want to talk about these. This mystery could make people think aliens are responsible for the UFOs.

When Venus is visible from Earth, ▶
it shines brightly in the night
sky. People might mistake
it for an alien ship.

UFOs can also
be bright space
objects, such as
the planet Venus
or a **meteor**. If
the night is cloudy
or foggy, it may be
hard to tell what these
things really are. Looking
at a light through glasses, windows, or camera
lenses can make it look unusual.

VENUS

MOON

Liquid water
can only exist
on planets in their
star's habitable zone.
Any closer, and the heat would
turn water to steam. Any farther away,
and the cold would turn water to ice.

CHAPTER THREE

SEARCHING FOR LIFE

There is no evidence that aliens have visited Earth. Could aliens live somewhere else in space? It is hard to know for sure. But scientists are working to find out.

So far, scientists know of just one place with life: Earth. To find more life, they are searching for other planets like Earth. These planets are around the same size as Earth. They are rocky, rather than made mostly of gas. And they are within their star's habitable zone. This is the distance away from a star where liquid water can exist. Life on Earth needs liquid water to survive. Finding planets in habitable zones may be our best chance of finding aliens.

KEPLER-22B **KEPLER-69C**

Scientists have found many planets outside our **solar system**. These are known as **exoplanets**. The first exoplanet found around a star like our sun was discovered in 1995. Since then, scientists have found thousands of exoplanets. But only some of these planets are similar to Earth. By 2019, scientists had found about 20 exoplanets in their star's habitable zone. If there are aliens out there, they may live on these planets.

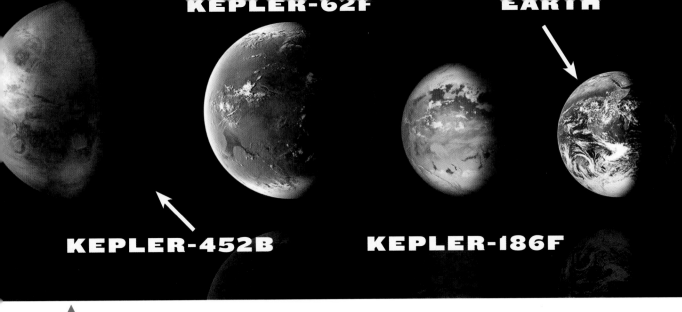

KEPLER-62F

EARTH

KEPLER-452B   KEPLER-186F

▲

This artist's illustration from NASA shows Earth with some of the known exoplanets similar to Earth.

DID YOU KNOW?

In 2019, scientists found the most Earthlike planets yet. They orbit a star called Teegarden's star. It is one of the closest stars to our sun. The planets are called Teegarden b and Teegarden c. They are similar to Earth in size, and they could likely have liquid water.

TALKING TO ALIENS

We don't know for sure if aliens are out there. But scientists have sent messages into space just in case. In the 1800s, people had ideas about flashing huge lights at Mars and Venus. Scientists later learned there was no life on these planets.

Some messages have been sent by spacecraft. *Pioneer 10* launched in 1972. *Pioneer 11* launched the next year. These spacecraft studied Jupiter and Saturn. Then they continued deeper into space. Scientists knew the spacecraft would go farther than any before. They would one day leave our solar system.

◀ *Pioneer 11* launched in 1973. Scientists knew *Pioneer 10* and *Pioneer 11* would travel far into outer space.

Scientists decided to include a golden **plaque** on each *Pioneer* spacecraft. The plaques showed a drawing of a man and a woman next to a drawing of the spacecraft. This would tell aliens how large humans are. The plaque also showed where our sun is compared to other stars. It showed which of the sun's planets the spacecraft came from. If aliens could read the plaque, they could find Earth.

DID YOU KNOW?

Another spacecraft message left Earth in 1977. *Voyager 1* and *Voyager 2* launched that year. They each carried a golden **record**. The record has recorded greetings in Earth languages. It has pictures from Earth. It even has Earth music.

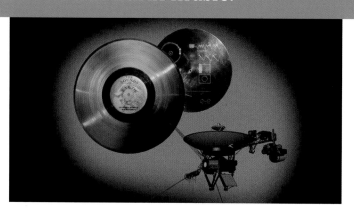

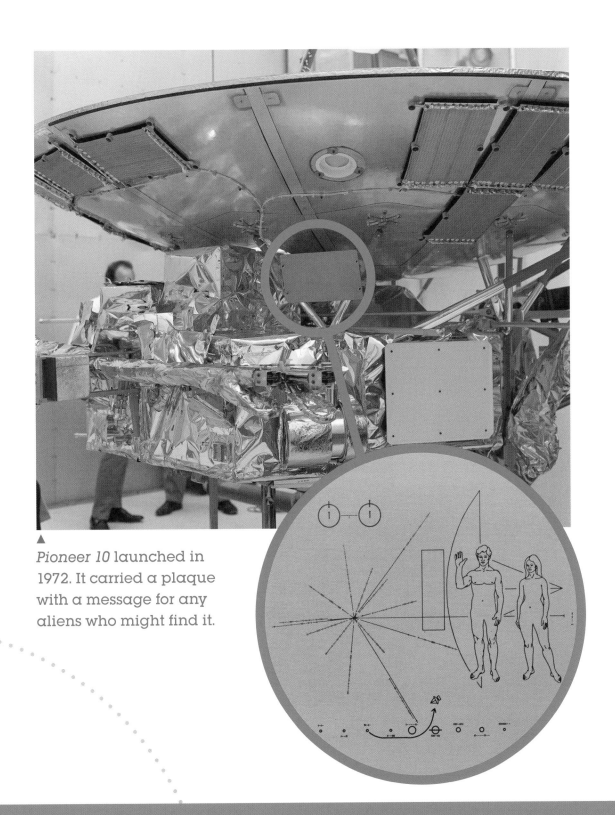

Pioneer 10 launched in 1972. It carried a plaque with a message for any aliens who might find it.

Other messages are sent by radio. These messages are special, and they can be turned into pictures. Scientists sent one of these messages in 1974. It came from a huge radio telescope in Arecibo, Puerto Rico. If aliens had an **antenna**, they could read the message and learn about Earth.

The message had a section about humans. Another section of the message had a map of the solar system. It showed the sun, the eight planets of our solar system, and Pluto. (Pluto was still called a planet in 1974.) The message could teach aliens about life on Earth.

Could aliens be sending similar messages to Earth? Scientists are listening. Antennas could pick up signals that are sent to Earth. Someday, people on Earth may hear from aliens.

Scientists sent the Arecibo message by radio in 1974. This graphic ▶ shows part of the message. The green section is about the human race. The pink section shows our solar system. The blue section is a drawing of the radio telescope that sent the message.

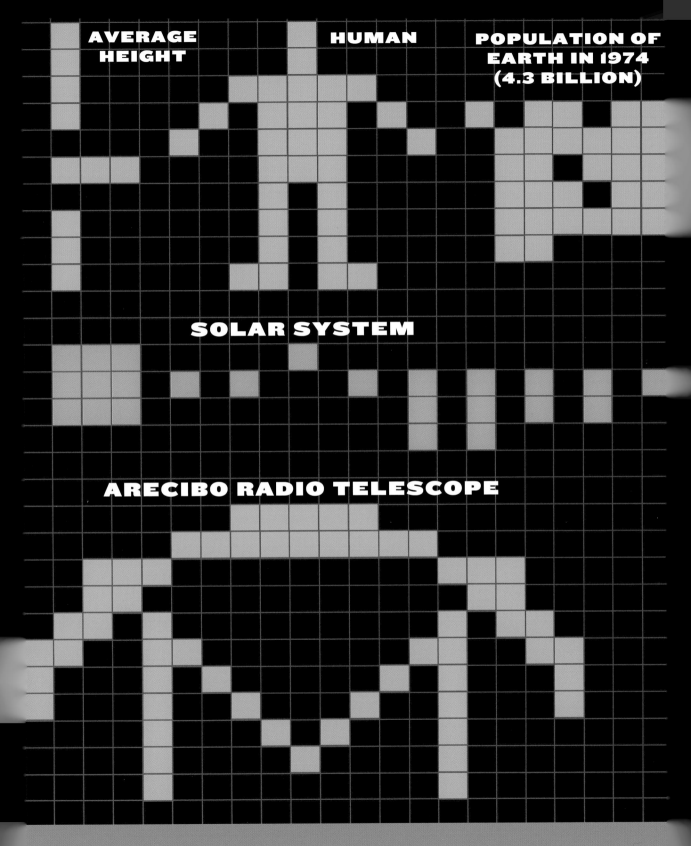

OUT OF THIS WORLD!

SETI

One of the biggest groups searching for alien life is called the SETI Institute. SETI stands for the Search for Extraterrestrial Intelligence. It was founded in 1984. The group listens for signals from space. It researches what alien life might be like. Finally, it also teaches the public about space science.

SETI uses the Allen Telescope Array to search for aliens. This collection of 42 antennas is in California. It can listen for signals seven days a week. Scientists can aim the antennas at several stars at a time. SETI is always listening, just in case aliens send a message.

▲

The SETI Institute's headquarters are in California. The institute works with NASA, the National Space Foundation, and other organizations.

◄ Allen Telescope Array

GLOSSARY

antenna (an-TEN-uh) An antenna is a machine that can send or receive radio signals. Scientists have used a powerful antenna to send messages into space.

exoplanets (EX-oh-plan-its) Exoplanets are planets found outside of our solar system. Scientists have discovered thousands of exoplanets.

meteor (MEE-tee-or) A meteor is a piece of rock or dust from space that comes close to Earth. A meteor burns up and shines brightly as it moves through the sky.

plaque (PLAK) A plaque is a piece of metal with writing or drawings on it. A plaque showing information about Earth is on *Pioneer 10* and *Pioneer 11*.

record (REK-ord) A record is a round object that stores information in tiny, thin grooves. A machine can read the grooves on a record to let people hear or see the information stored on it.

solar system (SOH-ler SIS-tum) The solar system includes the sun and all the objects near it, including planets and dwarf planets. No aliens have been found in our solar system.

TO LEARN MORE

IN THE LIBRARY

Higgins, Nadia. *UFOs*. Minneapolis, MN: Bellwether Media, 2014.

Kallio, Jamie. *Aliens*. Mankato, MN: The Child's World, 2016.

McClellan, Ray. *Alien Abductions*.
Minneapolis, MN: Bellwether Media, 2014.

ON THE WEB

Visit our website for links about UFOs and aliens:
childsworld.com/links

Note to Parents, Teachers, and Librarians: We routinely verify our Web links to make sure they are safe and active sites. So encourage your readers to check them out!

INDEX

aliens, 5–7, 9–10, 13–14, 17–20

Arecibo message, 20

Arnold, Kenneth, 5

exoplanets, 14

governments, 9–10

habitable zones, 13–14

Pioneer plaque, 18

Pioneer spacecraft, 17–18

Roswell, New Mexico, 6–7